WILDLIFE IN BLOOM SERIES

Little Badger

BY AUTHOR & CONSERVATIONIST

LINDA BLACKMOOR

ISBN: 978-1-966417-24-8 (PRINT)

PUBLISHED BY QUILL PRESS. LINDA BLACKMOOR'S TITLES MAY BE PURCHASED IN BULK FOR EDUCATIONAL, BUSINESS, FUNDRAISING, OR SALES PROMOTIONAL USE. FOR INFORMATION, PLEASE EMAIL HELLO@LINDABLACKMOOR.COM

FIRST PRINT EDITION: 2025

LINDA BLACKMOOR
WWW.LINDABLACKMOOR.COM

SPECIES

Badgers are small, sturdy mammals belonging to the Mustelidae family, which also includes weasels, otters, and wolverines. There are 11 different species of badgers spread across North America, Europe, Asia, and Africa. The most common types include the American badger, European badger, honey badger, and ferret-badger. Each species has unique adaptations that allow them to survive.

LOOKS

Badgers typically have stocky bodies, short legs, and long, sharp claws for digging. Their faces often display distinctive markings, such as the white stripes on the European badger's head. Coats can range from grayish to brown, with lighter undersides and bold facial patterns. Strong neck muscles help them use their jaws and claws with surprising force.

HABITAT

They inhabit woodlands, grasslands, farmlands, and deserts, preferring areas with loose soil for burrowing. The American badger thrives in the open prairies & plains of North America, while the European badger favors forests and farmland. Honey badgers can live in drier habitats, including savannas and scrublands of Africa and Southwest Asia. Shelter and food drive their choice of territory.

BURROWS

Badgers are skilled diggers that create underground homes called setts or dens, consisting of multiple tunnels and chambers. European badger setts can be incredibly complex, with dozens of entrances and passageways maintained by generations of badgers. Fresh bedding, like leaves and grass, is regularly carried into sleeping chambers. These burrows offer protection from predators and extreme weather.

DIET

Most badgers are omnivores, feasting on small mammals, insects, fruits, roots, and sometimes carrion. American badgers focus heavily on rodents like gophers and ground squirrels, often digging them out of burrows. Honey badgers eat snakes, rodents, and bee larvae, known for raiding beehives despite fierce stings. By controlling rodent and insect populations, badgers help maintain ecological balance.

BEHAVIOUR

Badgers have powerful front claws for excavating burrows and searching for prey underground. They can be solitary or live in family groups, depending on species and environment. Many are primarily nocturnal, venturing out at night to forage and retreating to their dens by day. Their robust bodies and fearless attitude allow them to defend territory and resources effectively.

SOCIAL

Social structures vary: the European badger often lives in groups called clans, sharing large setts and working together to maintain them. American badgers tend to be solitary, except during mating season or when mothers raise young. Honey badgers are mostly solitary too, famously independent and fierce when threatened. Social groupings influence how badgers cooperate or defend resources.

SENSES

A keen sense of smell is crucial for badgers to locate prey hidden underground or track mates. Their hearing is also sharp, picking up subtle movements of insects or rodents in the soil. Eyesight is less developed compared to other senses, but it's sufficient for nocturnal navigation. These heightened senses suit their digging lifestyle and nighttime habits.

DEFENSE

When threatened, badgers can hiss, growl, and bare their teeth, making themselves look larger and more intimidating. Their thick, loose skin allows them to twist around and bite attackers even when grabbed. Some species, like the honey badger, are notorious for their aggression and tenacity, driving away predators much larger than themselves. This fierce reputation helps deter most threats.

BABIES

Breeding seasons differ among species, but female badgers often delay implantation, meaning fertilized eggs pause development until conditions improve. After a gestation of 7 to 8 weeks (for American badgers) or longer with delayed implantation, 1 to 5 cubs (or kits) are born. Mothers nurse them underground until they're old enough to follow outside for food.

SLEEP

Badgers are known for digging special sleeping chambers lined with grass or leaves to keep warm and cozy. In colder climates, European badgers may enter a state of torpor, sleeping for longer periods to conserve energy during winter. American badgers stay active year-round, though they reduce activity in extreme cold. Safe, insulated dens are vital for resting and rearing offspring.

VOCALS

They communicate through vocalizations, scent marking, and body language to define territories and coordinate with group members. Scent marking involves rubbing scent glands on objects or depositing droppings in latrines near den entrances. Vocal calls range from growls and hisses to purr-like sounds when content. Clear communication helps maintain social bonds and protect resources from rivals.

BADGER FACTS #13

LIFESPAN

In the wild, badgers generally live 5 to 10 years, though some have survived longer under favorable conditions. Predation, road accidents, and habitat loss are major threats that can shorten their lifespans. In captivity, where threats are fewer, they may reach up to 14 years or more. Their ability to adapt and defend themselves contributes to their enduring presence across multiple continents.

www.ingramcontent.com/pod-product-compliance
Lightning Source LLC
Chambersburg PA
CBHW041346290326
41933CB00036B/109